A Brief History of the BANK OF EVERGLADES BUILDING

Marya Repko

ECITY • PUBLISHING

A Brief History of the Bank of Everglades Building

© 2021, text by Marya Repko
All rights reserved.

cover photo courtesy of Collier County Museums, Naples, FL (www.colliermuseums.com).
Historic photographs in this book are from the Florida State Archives unless otherwise noted.

set in Century Schoolbook, 12/16pt
printed & bound in the USA
First Edition, First Printing, May 2021

ABOUT THE TYPE FACE
The Century family of type was designed for Century Publishing in 1894 by typographer Linn Boyd Benton of American Type Founders and revised by his son Morris Fuller Benton. "Century Schoolbook" was commissioned in 1919 by textbook publisher Ginn & Co. and is known for its legibility.

ISBN 978-1-7341046-2-2

ECITY • PUBLISHING

P O Box 5033
Everglades City, FL, 34139
telephone (239) 695-2905
www.ecity-publishing.com

Other books from this publisher:
    A Brief History of the Everglades City Area
    The Story of Everglades City; A History for Younger Readers
    Historia de Everglades City (Spanish translation by Gloria Gutiérrez)
    A Brief History of the Fakahatchee
    A Brief History of Sanibel Island
    The Story of Sanibel Island; A History for Younger Readers
    Angel of the Swamp; Deaconess Harriet Bedell in the Everglades
    Grandma of the Glades; A Brief Biography of Marjory Stoneman Douglas
    Memories from Hadlyme; A Personal History of the East Haddam, CT, Area
    Women in the Everglades; Pioneers and Early Environmentalists
    The Story of Barron Collier; A History for Younger Readers
    Everglades Entrepreneur; Barron Gift Collier, Roaring Twenties Tycoon
    A Glance at History in the Everglades Area of Florida

A Brief History of the Bank of Everglades Building

PREFACE

This little book is dedicated to the volunteers and donors who are helping to restore the old Bank of Everglades Building.

The profits will benefit the "Save the Bank Fund".

A special thanks to my diligent proof-readers. Any errors are mine and I welcome hearing from readers with corrections, suggestions, and memories.

Marya Repko
Everglades City, FL
mrepko@earthlink.net
May, 2021

A Brief History of the Bank of Everglades Building

from a painting by Donald Sunshine

Artist Donald sunshine is professor emeritus of Architecture at Virginia Polytechnic but has spent numerous winters in southwest Florida, sketching local historic buildings.

He has given ESHP permission to use this picture to benefit the Bank of Everglades Building renovation effort.

A Brief History of the Bank of Everglades Building

CONTENTS

INTRODUCTION 1

BACKGROUND HISTORY 3

COLLIER AND HIS COUNTY 5

THE BUSINESS AND THE PEOPLE 11

NEW BEGINNINGS 13

BED & BREAKFAST 17

THE FUTURE 19

FURTHER READING 20

TIMELINE 21

A Brief History of the Bank of Everglades Building

Florida in 1859. The Everglades area was in Monroe County whose seat was Key West. In 1887 Lee County was established and in 1923 Collier County was formed. The newer counties included the village of Everglade.

A Brief History of the Bank of Everglades Building

INTRODUCTION

Everglades City on the fringe of the swamp is fortunate in preserving its historical heritage for almost 100 years. As you walk or drive around the peaceful streets, you can see original cottage homes, lovingly restored by proud owners.

Public buildings that have also been saved are City Hall (the original Collier County Courthouse), the Laundry (now Museum of the Everglades), the Masonic Lodge plus the famous Rod & Gun Club which dates from the 1870s. Down in Chokoloskee, the island four miles south of the City, the Smallwood Store looks almost the same as when it was built a hundred years ago and serves as a popular Museum, thanks to the foresight of the founder's granddaughter.

To learn more about our area's unique history, see www.evergladeshistorical.org, the website of the Everglades Society for Historic Preservation (ESHP) founded in 2004 by local concerned citizens as a 501(c)(3) not-for-profit corporation to save the old Courthouse, which was rescued by FEMA after Hurricane Wilma. The Society has since fostered pride in our heritage by erecting signage in front of buildings and holding events focused on local history.

A Brief History of the Bank of Everglades Building

One building whose future is a work-in-progress is the old Bank of Everglades Building, a landmark on the central Broadway avenue. The Bank's history is checkered but there is hope for its future. In March 2021, the owner generously donated the Building to ESHP who is working to renovate it.

The plan is for the Building to house the Visitor Center downstairs with space for community events and to rent the rooms upstairs as artists' studios, small specialty shops, or professional business offices to create jobs and opportunities in the community.

The task is daunting – repair the foundation and install a new roof, windows, elevator, air conditioning, and then tackle interior rehabilitation.

Along with major fundraising, including grants and events, profits from this little book are donated to the "Save the Bank Fund".

Donors can make a tax-deductible contribution using a credit/debit card on the dedicated website www.SaveBoE.com or send a check payable to "ESHP" with a memo line "Save the Bank" to
    ESHP
    P O Box 46
    Everglades City, FL, 34139

A Brief History of the Bank of Everglades Building

BACKGROUND HISTORY

The first documented inhabitants in southwest Florida were the Calusa tribe who built shell mounds that we still see today. They lived along the coast when Spanish sailors explored "La Florida" from 1513 onwards.

By the 1850s the territory belonged to the United States and the Everglades was populated sparsely by members of Seminole tribes fleeing from deportation to west of the Mississippi River.

When the Civil War ended in 1865, white farmers sailed along the coasts and rivers looking for a warm climate. One early explorer was C.S. (Ted) Smallwood who built a trading post on the island of Chokoloskee to serve the small local population as well as the Seminoles from the hinterland who sold skins and meat in exchange for ammunition and colorful cloth to make patchwork shirts and skirts.

The Ted Smallwood Store in Chokoloskee is now a Museum.
photo courtesy Florida State Archives

A Brief History of the Bank of Everglades Building

The store has been preserved as a Museum by Ted's granddaughter Lynn and welcomes visitors daily.

Another intrepid family was the Storters who built houses along the river in what was named Everglade when it was granted a Post Office in 1893. They grew sugar cane that was reduced to syrup and sold in Key West, a major shipping port. The area also produced vegetables (e.g., tomatoes, cucumbers) which were appreciated by northern markets in winter. The original Storter homestead is now the famous Rod & Gun Club.

The Storter home on the River in Everglades City, 1915.
photo courtesy Florida State Archives

This remote rural region was self-sufficient and usually independent of outside interference until the early 1920s when it was discovered by Barron Gift Collier.

A Brief History of the Bank of Everglades Building

COLLIER AND HIS COUNTY

Barron Gift Collier was born on March 23, 1873, in Memphis, Tennessee, to a middle-class family. His father Myles had served in the Confederate Navy and named his second son after two officers: Samuel Barron and George Gift.

Young Barron left school at 16 and sold gas-powered street lighting until he saw the need for clean and timely advertising in the new electric street cars. He provided this service by printing standard-sized cards that could be slotted easily into frames.

Street Car Advertising Cards supplied by Barron Collier.
photo from www.historic-memphis.com

He was known for his reliability and the business spread all over the southern states until he expanded to New York City in 1905, already a millionaire at an early age.

A Brief History of the Bank of Everglades Building

One of his potential customers was John Roach from Chicago who had a vacation home on Useppa, the island west of Fort Myers on the Gulf Coast of Florida. Collier visited there and bought the property. He saw a great future for the state and continued purchases of land until he owned over one million acres in the southwest.

Unfortunately, the only access to his holdings was by boat. Construction of the road planned from Tampa to Miami (the "Tamiami Trail") halted in World War I for lack of money and manpower. Collier promised to fund its completion through the swamp if a county were formed from his land. In 1923, Collier County was established and its go-getter "Daddy" selected the little village of Everglade as his headquarters because of the central location and wide river which he renamed after himself.

Everglades (Collier added the final "s" to the name) was laid out as a planned town with a grid of streets centered on the Circle (a bit like Washington, DC, or Paris). Among the amenities he provided were the County Courthouse and a library, school, laundry, inn with department store downstairs, theater, and bank.

Everglades City in 1931 with grid of streets and circle at center.
courtesy of Collier County Museums, Naples, FL

A Brief History of the Bank of Everglades Building

The latter was founded in 1923 as the "State Bank of Everglades" and housed in several little wooden buildings at the west end of Broadway.

The little Bank of Everglades Building near the Post Office.
courtesy of Collier County Museums, Naples, FL

The first President was Barron's older brother C.M. ("Uncle Charlie") who acted as his right-hand man throughout the development of Collier's business here and in New York.

Another trusted helper was William O. Sparklin, the architect who designed not only the Courthouse and the Everglades Laundry building but the new Bank Building in the neo-classical style. They are all are listed in the National Register of Historic Places where Sparklin is named as responsible for five properties in southwest Florida (two in Lee County are the schools in Olga and Tice).

And, many of them were built by the Sparklin-Gift Construction Company, proof of how close the two men were.

A Brief History of the Bank of Everglades Building

Neo-classical design of the County Courthouse and the Bank.
courtesy of Collier County Museums, Naples, FL

The Bank of Everglades moved into its new dignified headquarters in 1927. There were offices above the Bank for the *Collier County News* which became the *Naples News* in 1963 after it moved. It was also home to the Inter-County Telephone & Telegraph Company and the Collier-Hendry Title Company.

The Bank survived the 1929 stock market crash but Collier was eventually declared bankrupt in 1933 when his borrowings exceeded his liquidity. Although he had substantial property holdings, no one could afford to buy them in the depressed economy.

Collier himself only survived a few more years. He suffered heart problems during a visit to his beloved Useppa and was rushed by train to New York City where he died in hospital on March 13, 1939.

He was succeeded by his wife Juliet Carnes and sons Barron, Jr., Sam, and Miles but the two younger men died early, leaving responsibility for the businesses to Barron, Jr., who was helped by David Graham Copeland.

A Brief History of the Bank of Everglades Building

Sam, Miles, D.G. Copeland, and Barron, Jr. in the Rod & Gun.
courtesy of Collier County Museums, Naples, FL

After Gulf Oil failed to find oil in the Big Cypress, the Building housed offices in the 1940s for the Humble Oil Company (now Exxon-Mobil) who were successful in the Sunniland field about 30 miles north of Everglades. One of the Humble employees in 1945 to 1950 was Gene Davidson who settled and brought up his family here.

The District School Board also had an office in the Building and another office was the home of the Collier & Long Insurance Agency operated by Barron's cousin C.H. Collier, an officer in the Bank.

A Brief History of the Bank of Everglades Building

Top: Barron Gift Collier, official portrait, 1912.
courtesy of Florida State Archives
Bottom: Charles Myles (C.M.) Collier, Barron's elder brother..
courtesy of Collier County Museums, Naples, FL

A Brief History of the Bank of Everglades Building

THE BUSINESS & THE PEOPLE

The President of the Bank in 1927 is recorded as C.M. Collier and the Chief Cashier was Joseph M. Bryan who built a house on Riverside Drive in Everglades and later became the first President who was not a member of the Collier family.

The Vice-President in 1927 was Daniel McLeod, the County Tax Assessor and Mayor of Everglades for almost 50 years, after whom our little park is named.

In 1954 the Bank claimed in a flyer that their deposits were almost $2 million. It was FDIC insured and there were safe deposit boxes to rent. The President was C.H. Collier.

An advertisement in the October 24, 1956, edition of the *Ft Myers News-Press*, proudly boasted:

Newly Remodeled ... Newly Enlarged
Progressive Growth!

In keeping with Everglades' steady, progressive growth, Bank of Everglades has recently remodeled and enlarged their banking facilities.

Distinctive changes have been made to the interior of the bank to provide better service for you. An addition was also made in the rear of the building.

This is your personal invitation to stop in and see the newly remodeled and newly enlarged Bank of Everglades.

A Brief History of the Bank of Everglades Building

At that time, J.L. Howell was President and one of the Vice-Presidents was Mildred Cooke who moved in 1944 to Everglades where she met her husband Paul, a realtor and later a City Councilman.

Several local women remember working in the Bank with Mrs. Cooke in the 1950s. She was later elected as Mayor of Everglades City in 1973 and served for two years, the first and only woman to do so.

The interior of the Bank with an old sketch found in the Building.

A Brief History of the Bank of Everglades Building

NEW BEGINNINGS

A referendum in 1959 decided to move the County seat to Naples which had become much more populous with the development of resort hotels along the beaches and businesses. The new Government Center, built on a greenfield site in East Naples, was ready in 1962 and officials left Everglades City. The old Courthouse became City Hall but still houses branches of the County library, tax collector, and planning department.

However, before the re-location, the whole area was devastated in 1960, by Hurricane Donna which flooded the City with over 8-feet of muddy water from the storm surge. It is said that money from the Bank was hung out to dry and not one note was stolen.

Destruction to the wooden buildings on Broadway east of the Bank in what is now McLeod Park after Hurricane Wilma in 1960.
photo courtesy Florida State Archives

A Brief History of the Bank of Everglades Building

It was decided to move the financial business to Immokalee, a market town about 40 miles north, and was renamed the First Bank of Immokalee in 1965. The town was headquarters of the Collier Corporation which still had multiple land-holdings and interests in agriculture.

The old Bank of Everglades Building was converted into a boarding house.

The next significant owner was William "Buck" Dawson, a colorful and ambitious man who established the Swimming Hall of Fame in Fort Lauderdale in 1964.

Dawson had big plans for the Bank of Everglades Building and is quoted by *Sports Illustrated* on April 29, 1974:

> "This is where I'd live if I had my druthers," Dawson told some locals in the cafe. "In the meantime, I'm going to make that bank into a tourist attraction. It'll include a Presidential Fishing Hall of Fame and the world's largest collection of stuffed fish."

Dawson even met with Mayor Mildred Cooke in 1974 to discuss the Jetport planned by the Miami-Dade Port Authority in the Big Cypress, about 30 miles east of Everglades City on the Trail. Although local people were enthusiastic about the jobs this massive development could bring as the largest Supersonic Airport in the country, it was opposed by environmentalists who argued that paving over the

A Brief History of the Bank of Everglades Building

land would stop water flow into Everglades National Park and disturb wildlife. Construction of the Jetport was stopped after only one runway was built and Big Cypress National Preserve was created.

Dawson also bought the old Everglades Inn which tragically burned down in 1987. Unfortunately, he did not achieve his goals here.

Joe & Reba ("Rusty') Rupsis bought the Bank of Everglades Building in 1979. They had operated radio stations and were living in Clewiston when the idea of a newspaper was suggested because Everglades City was too small to support a broadcaster.

It was Rusty who founded, edited, and published the *Everglades Echo*, a weekly tabloid full of local information and advertising for only 15-cents. The masthead was drawn by local artist Camille Baumgartner.

In the days before one could just send a computer file, she drove up to Immokalee with her pasted-up layout, waited while it was made into plates for the printing presses, and then dashed home to distribute copies.

A Brief History of the Bank of Everglades Building

Rusty Rupsis putting the *Everglades Echo* to bed.
from the Fort Myers News-Press, September 28, 1988

Rusty and Joe lived in the Building and also operated a boarding house there until they retired in 1988 and moved away.

The newspaper was taken over by the Tuff group before another publisher from Naples closed it completely. *The Mullet Rapper*, started in October 2006 by Patty Huff, now provides our news and events calendar. The current owner, publisher, and editor of the *Rapper* is Kathy Brock who makes digital copies available at www.VisitEvergladesCity.com.

A Brief History of the Bank of Everglades Building

BED & BREAKFAST

The next owner to make any significant changes was Robert Flick who bought the building in 1996. His daughter Patty had some internal remodeling done and opened a Bed & Breakfast in December 1997. That was quite successful and advertised "breakfast in the vault" for guests.

Patty Flick was proud of the Building and applied for it to be added to the National Register of Historic Places in 1999.

The business was taken over by Cheryl Henderson and Claudia Davenport in 2003. Besides lodging, it offered extensive spa treatments, a gift shop specializing in natural beauty products, and guided tours of the area. They moved from the area in 2008.

Patty Bowen, part owner of the Rod & Gun Club, re-opened the B&B in October 2011 and filled the rooms with antique furniture, advertising the "Everglades Historical Bed & Breakfast with Spa" but finally closed in 2017.

A Brief History of the Bank of Everglades Building

Artist Hannah Ineson is known for her watercolors, pottery, and clever drawings. She lives in Maine most of the year but enjoys winters in Florida where she is active in the community.

She sketched the Bank of Everglades Building from historic photos to benefit the renovation effort.

SAVE THE HISTORIC BANK OF EVERGLADES BUILDING
www.SaveBoE.com

A Brief History of the Bank of Everglades Building

THE FUTURE

The building was vacant for six months when Hurricane Irma struck in September 2017, leaving the usual grey mucky flood water.

The black historical plaque in front of the Building was erected in 2014 by ESHP and tells the story of the Bank.

The Building was named as one of the "11 to Save" in 2018 by the Florida Trust for Historic Preservation who had sent an architect to evaluate hurricane damage around the City.

In March 2021, owner Bob Flick handed over the Building to ESHP and can rest assured that its future is in good hands.

FURTHER READING

BOOKS

Andrews, Allen H., **A Yank Pioneer in Florida**, 1950: Douglas Printing Co, Jacksonville, FL

Dorsey Tim, **Hurricane Punch**, 2007: William Morrow, New York, NY.

Friends of the Museum of the Everglades, **Historic Buildings Around Everglades City; Walking Tours,** 2006: FME, Everglades City, FL.

Repko, Marya, **Everglades Entrepreneur; Barron Gift Collier, Roaring Twenties Tycoon,** 2018: ECity Publishing, Everglades City, FL

Repko, Marya, **A Brief History of the Everglades City Area,** 2005: ECity Publishing, Everglades City, FL

Tebeau, Charlton W, **Florida's Last Frontier: The History of Collier County,** 1966: University of Miami Press, Miami, FL.

WEBSITES

www.colliermuseums.com *County Museum Archives*
www.floridamemory.com *Florida State Archives*
www.hathaitrust.org *archive of periodicals*
www.historic-memphis.com *photos of Collier family*
www.newspapers.com *newspaper archives*

A Brief History of the Bank of Everglades Building

TIMELINE

- 1513 Spanish discovered Florida
- 1821 United States gained territory of Florida
- 1869 William Smith Allen farmed in Everglades
- 1881 Storter family farmed in Everglades
- 1911 Barron Collier bought Useppa
- 1923 Collier County was established
- 1927 Bank moved into new Building
- 1928 Tamiami Trail completed
- 1939 Barron Collier died
- 1953 Everglades incorporated as a City
- 1960 Hurricane Donna
- 1962 County seat moved to East Naples
- 1962 Bank business moved to Immokalee
- 1970s Buck Dawson owned Building
- 1979 Rupsis owned Building, published "Echo"
- 1997 Bob Flick & daughter Patty opened B&B
- 1999 Building listed on National Register
- 2003 Claudia & Cheryl operated B&B with spa
- 2011 Patty Bowen operated Historic B&B
- 2017 Building unused, for sale
- 2017 Hurricane Irma
- 2018 Building nominated as "11 to Save"
- 2021 Building donated to ESHP

www.ingramcontent.com/pod-product-compliance
Lightning Source LLC
Chambersburg PA
CBHW071256070526
44583CB00017B/2500